The SPORTS HEROES Library

Football's STEADIEST KICKERS

Nathan Aaseng

Lerner Publications Company • Minneapolis

To Dave

LIBRARY OF CONGRESS CATALOGING IN PUBLICATION DATA

Aaseng, Nathan.
  Football's steadiest kickers.

  (The Sports heroes library)
  SUMMARY: Traces the careers of eight NFL kickers whose last-second goals have decided many crucial games. Includes Lou Groza, George Blanda, Fred Cox, Tom Dempsey, Garo Yepremian, Efren Herrera, Rolf Benirschke, and Tony Franklin.

  1. Placekickers (Football)—United States—Biography—Juvenile literature. 2. National Football League—Juvenile literature. [1. Football players] I. Title.
  GV939.A1A177   796.332′092′2 [B] [920]   80-28863
  ISBN 0-8225-1069-3

Copyright © 1981 by Lerner Publications Company

All rights reserved. International copyright secured. No part of this book may be reproduced in any form whatsoever without permission in writing from the publisher except for the inclusion of brief quotations in an acknowledged review.

Manufactured in the United States of America.

International Standard Book Number: 0-8225-1069-3
Library of Congress Catalog Card Number: 80-28863

1 2 3 4 5 6 7 8 9 10 90 89 88 87 86 85 84 83 82 81

Contents

	Introduction	5
1	Lou Groza	9
2	George Blanda	17
3	Fred Cox	27
4	Tom Dempsey	35
5	Garo Yepremian	45
6	Efren Herrera	55
7	Rolf Benirschke	63
8	Tony Franklin	71

Seattle's Efren Herrera rests on the sidelines. Like all kickers, Herrera spends a lot of time watching the game and waiting for the chance to help his team with a kick.

Introduction

When you think about it, "football" sounds like a strange name for a game in which only two players on a team ever kick the ball. In fact, outside of punting and placekicking, a team can be *penalized* for kicking the ball while it is in play.

When football first started, however, it was meant to be more of a kicking game. In 1884 the scoring rules awarded two points for a touchdown, *four* points for the after-touchdown kick, and five points for a field goal. The scoring in football has changed a lot since then, but one thing has not changed. Many games are still won and lost with the swing of a foot.

The men who make these important field goals seem as out of place on a football field as a mechanic would be working in a suit and tie. Some are scarcely more than half the size of the men who block for them. And some even know very little about the game they are playing. But most striking of all, on a grass field the placekickers are the only ones with clean uniforms!

Because they are such a different part of the game, placekickers are often the game's forgotten people. Few youngsters who dream of becoming football stars ever choose placekicker as their favorite position. In fact, most of the stars in this book began kicking by accident. Kickers are almost never chosen until the later rounds of the college draft. Even at practice, they often just pass the time until the other players leave the field. Then when everyone else is done practicing, placekickers go out with the center and holder to practice. Sometimes these kickers stay practicing their art until the sun has gone down.

A kicker's main task is to boot a football from the ground through a target that is 18 feet, 6 inches wide and 10 feet off of the ground. In the late 1960s and early 1970s, these players became so skilled at their job that they were almost spoiling the fun of football. Many teams would spend a whole game knocking each other down around midfield and then let the kickers do the scoring.

Fred Cox of the Vikings boots one from a Paul Krause hold.

An offense had only to cross the 50-yard line to be within range of these powerful legs.

In 1974 the rulemakers decided something had to be done about this. They pushed the goalposts back from the front of the end zone to the back, which added 10 yards to every kick. They also declared that if the ball had been hiked beyond the 20-yard line, the defense would get the ball from the original line of scrimmage instead of at the 20-yard line if a field goal try was unsuccessful. This made coaches think twice about trying long field goals and giving up good field position.

This new rule made the placekicker's job tougher than before and also made it much more likely for the kicker to miss an important field goal. When a game was close and 70,000 fans expected a kicker to come through, that could be a very uncomfortable situation for him. If a kicker failed to come through, he could ruin the work of his entire team.

Today not many players can stand up to that kind of pressure, and several new placekickers bounce in and out of the National Football League (NFL) each year. But a successful kicker can enjoy a career twice as long as that of most of his teammates. And the longer he plays, the more points he piles up and the more famous he becomes. A placekicker with a successful record can give his team a strong edge on its opponents. His teammates know that if they give him a chance, he will come through and win the game for them. Here are eight kickers that any coach would have loved to have trying the game-winning kicks for his team.

1
Lou Groza

When Lou Groza started playing pro football in 1946, the goalposts were little more than pieces of wood that players sometimes ran into. In those days, coaches expected touchdowns, not field goals. Then many teams tried as few as five or six field goals in an entire season. The goalposts, of course, were used for the point after touchdown, but even that was not considered very important. So most teams gave the job of placekicking to a regular offensive player.

But by the time Lou retired in 1965, however, placekickers had practically taken over the game. These specialists, whose only job in the game was to placekick, began to lead the league in scoring. One of the major reasons for the change was Groza's magic toe.

During his 21-year career with the Cleveland Browns, Lou "The Toe" Groza was football's leading kicker.

Lou was born in Martin's Ferry, Ohio, in 1924. Although Lou finally grew to be 6 feet, 3 inches tall and 250 pounds, he was the smallest boy in his family. It was Lou's older brother, Frank, who got Lou interested in kicking a football. When they were young, the two would practice for hours, using the telephone wires by the high school as their crossbar. By the time he was 14, Lou's right leg became so powerful that he could boot the ball 60 yards.

At that time, it was unheard of for anyone to be "just a kicker." So in high school, Lou gained more respect for his play as a lineman than for his kicking. Lou was not only the captain of his high school football team; he also showed his all-around skill by leading the basketball and baseball teams.

When Groza finished high school in 1942, he followed his brother Frank to Ohio State University. There Lou played in only three games before he was called into the army. But during his brief time at the school, he had impressed his coach, Paul Brown. And Brown managed to keep track of this fine athlete even though Groza spent the next several years of World War II far away in the Pacific Ocean.

When Lou finally left the service in 1946, Coach Brown was waiting for him with helmet and uniform.

But instead of coaching at Ohio State, Brown was now the head coach of the brand-new Cleveland Browns pro football team. So Lou decided to go with Brown instead of continuing at Ohio State.

From the very start, the Cleveland Browns ran all over the other teams in the All-American Football Conference. If it wasn't fullback Marion Motley thundering through the line for huge gains, it was quarterback Otto Graham throwing for touchdowns. During his first years with Cleveland, Groza worked mostly on his placekicking. The Browns had him trying long kicks that no one else would even dream of attempting. During one game, Coach Brown was wondering aloud if Groza could make a 51-yard field goal. He was a little surprised when Groza told him it would be no problem. When Lou went out and swung his leg into the ball, the opposing Chicago Rocket players who had tried to block the kick turned to watch it. When it cleared the crossbar, one of them was so impressed with the kick that he went up to Lou and shook his hand.

In 1948 Lou broke into the starting lineup at offensive tackle. And with his help, the Browns became better than ever. They were actually too good for their opposition, and the other teams in the league began to go out of business. Cleveland

Paul Brown coached Groza at Ohio State and later brought Lou to Cleveland. There Groza became one of Brown's most dependable players.

then joined the rival National Football League in 1950. The NFL teams were eager to prove they were far better than anyone from that other league. And the Browns were just as determined to show that they were the best team in football. The Browns quickly proved they deserved their reputation when they earned a spot in the championship game against the Los Angeles Rams. The game was a tense, hard-hitting one, played in freezing weather, and neither team was able to hold on to the lead for very long. Then with 1 minute, 48 seconds left, the Browns trailed, 28-27, and the ball was 68 long yards away from a touchdown. Oddly, it had been the Browns' strong kicking that had caused them to be behind. A strong gust of wind had spoiled the hike from center on the try for an extra point attempt that would have tied the game.

The Browns still had such faith in their kicking game that they hardly worried about scoring a touchdown. Calmly they marched downfield while the game drew to a close. There were only 20 seconds left when Lou dropped back to try the field goal. The snap from center was on target, and Lou kicked the 16-yard field goal that made the Browns the champions of the NFL.

Lou's success under pressure continued the following year. Then he kicked a 51-yard field goal in the play-offs to top the old play-off record by 10 yards. It was not enough, however, to beat the Rams that year.

Lou's reliable placekicking made him so famous that he was known as "The Toe." His kicks made many people forget he was probably just as good an offensive lineman as he was a kicker. From

1951 to 1955, his crushing blocks earned him All-Pro honors for five straight years, and he was named All-Pro again in 1957. In each of those years, Groza played an important role in helping Cleveland to win their conference championship and also the league title in 1954 and 1955.

In 1960 Lou hurt his back so seriously that he sat out the entire year. Many thought the 36-year old would retire for good. While it turned out that he was through blocking for Cleveland, he could still kick as well as anyone in the league. Lou went on to score over 600 points after his "retirement." In fact, he enjoyed his best season in 1964 and scored 115 points. Finally, after years of fighting off the younger kickers who were trying to beat him out of a job, Lou called it quits after the 1965 season. In his 21 years in pro football, he led the league in field goals five times. He had also scored 1,608 total points. It was not until a decade later that his record was topped by George Blanda.

In 1974 Lou received a thrill when he was named to the Hall of Fame. That award was a fitting honor for the man who had helped to show the effect a good kicker could have in a football game. More than any other player, The Toe had put the "foot" back into football.

George Blanda, football's all-time scoring leader, starred as both a quarterback and kicker through 26 professional seasons.

2
George Blanda

The average pro football player is lucky to last five years in the National Football League. And even the best and sturdiest of players are usually happy to call it quits by age 38. Then there was George Blanda, the man writers called the dinosaur of pro football. Many of his teammates were not even born when George started playing pro ball. In fact, Blanda did not really make it big until he was well past the age of 40!

George was born in 1927 in Youngwood, Pennsylvania, 1 of 11 children of a poor coal miner. George helped the family's finances by setting up pins in a bowling alley and trapping muskrats.

During high school, Blanda starred in football as a halfback and a kicker. His leg was so strong he could kick the ball over the goalposts on kickoffs. George not only starred on the track team as well: he *was* the track team. From reading books, he learned to put the shot and toss the javelin and the discus, and at meets he would be the only one entered from his school. Oddly enough, the most serious accident Blanda suffered in sports was not in football but in track and field. At one track meet, George was struck in the leg by a javelin.

The javelin wound not only hurt George, it may also have cost him a scholarship to Notre Dame University. He was still limping around after his accident when a Notre Dame coach came to Youngwood, intending to offer George a scholarship. Because the man was not impressed with the slow-moving Blanda, he left without making him the offer. And Blanda enrolled at the University of Kentucky instead of at Notre Dame.

After a discouraging 1-9 record during his freshman year at Kentucky, Blanda wondered why he had ever left home. But when Paul Bryant took over as coach the next season, the team improved. Bryant also taught George some lessons in discipline. Blanda was feeling pretty important after starring in a Kentucky win. But during practice a few days later, he made one small mistake. The "star" then found himself running laps around the track until the sun went down.

In 1949 George joined the Chicago Bears as a modest 12th-round draft choice. Unknown to him at the time, that draft would be the start of 10 strange years of frustration for him. To many people, Blanda seemed to be just what the Bears needed at quarterback. But George did not get along at all with the Bears' head coach, George Halas. Even though Blanda almost always came through when he was given a chance, he was rarely given a second chance. At one point, the frustrated 215-pound quarterback moved over to the defense. At least as a linebacker he had gotten a chance to play. The situation with the Bears got so bad that in 1959, Blanda was actually paid to sit out the year!

By 1960 George was a 31-year-old quarterback with practically no experience. Fortunately he was able to escape the Bears when the new American Football League (AFL) was formed that year. Halas, convinced that the new league would not last long, allowed Blanda to try his luck there. Suddenly the unwanted quarterback found himself *very* wanted. The AFL teams were all jumping at the chance to land a real quarterback from the NFL.

George enjoyed the special attention for a while and finally chose to play for the Houston Oilers. He immediately showed what he could do if he was only given a chance. He passed and kicked the Oilers to the championship in the league's first two seasons.

George, however, was already thought of as old for a quarterback. So when the Oilers started to lose a few years later, the fans blamed the losses on Blanda's age. Then when a sore arm caused George to have a subpar season in 1966, he was quickly dropped from the Oiler team. It seemed as though the end had finally come for the grizzled 39-year-old passer.

But the Oakland Raiders did not agree and thought they might be able to get another one or two good playing years out of George. The Raiders were more interested in Blanda's kicking leg than in his passing arm. So for the next few seasons, Blanda quietly played back-up quarterback and did the placekicking for the rapidly improving Raiders. Few people even noticed that his kicking was bringing him to within reach of the NFL all-time scoring records. (By then the AFL had become a part of the NFL.)

But in 1970 even the Raiders decided that

Blanda's passing and kicking won many last-minute victories for the Raiders. Here Kenny Stabler holds for a Blanda kick.

George was through. When he was put on waivers, not one other team wanted him. But George received one last chance when the young Raider kickers failed to come through that year. Blanda rejoined the team, and the old kicker won the Western Division title of the AFC for Oakland.

As the Raiders faced the Pittsburgh Steelers, their record stood at 2-2-1. After such a slow start, the Raiders could not afford another loss so soon. But they were only tied with the Steelers when Raider quarterback Daryl Lamonica went out with an injury. Oakland then sent in their 43-year-old back-up quarterback. George shocked Pittsburgh by unloading three touchdown passes—two to tight end Raymond Chester—to win the game, 31-14.

The next week, Lamonica took over again at quarterback. But as the final seconds of the game were ticking away, the Raiders trailed, 17-14. Their only hope was if somehow Blanda could kick a 48-yard field goal into a strong wind. When George trotted out on the field, he saw the Kansas City Chiefs' 6-foot, 10-inch Morris Stroud and 6-foot, 7-inch Buck Buchanon waiting to bat down the kick. So he knew he would have to boot the ball high as well as far. George stepped into the ball and swung his leg. The ball cleared the crossbar by a few feet, and the Raiders earned a tie!

One week later, Lamonica was hurt again. With less than two minutes left in that game, Oakland trailed the Cleveland Browns, 20-13. But Blanda threw a touchdown pass to tie the game. Then the Raiders intercepted a Cleveland pass. Again there were just three seconds left as Blanda went out to try an important long field goal. This one would have to be for 52 yards. Could Blanda do it again? He did and turned yet another Oakland loss into a 23-20 victory.

By this time, football fans around the country were watching to see how long George could keep on saving the Raiders. It was almost too much to believe when the Denver Broncos pulled ahead, 19-17, with a few minutes left to play. Again George took over. Standing up to a ferocious Bronco pass rush, he marched his team downfield all the way from the Oakland 20-yard line. Touchdown! Oakland won again! By this time Blanda had become the hero of middle-aged Americans everywhere.

The Raiders made Blanda's fifth straight game saver a little easier the next week when they played the San Diego Chargers. They drove deep into the Chargers' territory in the final minutes and left Blanda with a 16-yard kick. Compared to the last few weeks, that little kick was almost boring for Blanda as his field goal broke a 17-17 tie for yet another Oakland win. Blanda nearly pulled off a sixth straight miracle finish against the Detroit Lions the following week, but he was stopped by a key off-sides penalty.

Young George Blanda of the Chicago Bears

While experts marveled at the "old-timer," the gruff Blanda did not even want to be called old. He thought all of the fuss about his age was a lot of baloney. If a person worked hard, stayed in shape, and gave it his best, Blanda said, he saw no reason why he could not play until he was 50.

And George nearly did make it to age 50. But he was finally dropped from the team before the

George in a Raider uniform many years later

1976 season. By that time, Blanda held nearly all of the scoring records in the NFL. His records include the most years as a pro—26, the most points in a career—2,002, and the most field goals—335.

The Chicago Bears must wince whenever they see George Blanda's name listed after all of those records. Talk about having the last laugh!

25

Fred Cox, Minnesota's all-time scoring leader, follows through on a warm-up kick before a Vikings' game.

3
Fred Cox

Ask a pro football fan if he remembers Fred Cox, the power runner, and the fan will probably give you a very funny look. Very likely he or she will tell you that you must have Cox confused with someone else. Nearly every football fan knows that Fred Cox was the old reliable placekicker for the Minnesota Vikings. It is hard to even picture this quiet, businesslike man in the Number 14 uniform even touching a football with his hands, much less running with it.

But when Fred was drafted into pro football, he had no thoughts of being a placekicker. At that point in his career, he had only booted a handful of field goals. It was an injury that would turn Fred into the kicker who would help to win the close games for the Vikings.

Fred was born in Monongahela, Pennsylvania, in 1938. After his first experience as a kicker, it is little wonder that kicking was not his first love. As a high school sophomore, Fred was sent in to try a kick. He swung his foot into the ball and watched it dribble about 12 yards downfield as if all of the air had been let out of it. Since a teammate recovered the ball, many thought Fred had kicked it that way on purpose. But the embarrassed Fred knew better and figured he had better stick to being a running back.

Cox moved on to the University of Pittsburgh in 1957. There he gained many tough yards as a straight-ahead runner, and he impressed a number of pro teams by leading the team in rushing. His performance impressed the Cleveland Browns who claimed him as a future draft choice in the eighth round of the 1961 draft. That meant the Browns held the rights to Fred even though he had a year of college left.

Shortly after he received the news from the Browns, Fred injured his back. This was probably one of the most important events in Fred's career. Now he knew he would have to work on his placekicking if he ever wanted to play pro football. And the experience also convinced Cox to become a chiropractor, one who treats back problems.

Because of his injury, Fred knew it would not be easy to make it in the pros. His job was especially tough because the Browns already had Lou Groza, the best kicker in the game. So Fred gave his best in practice and made Groza work hard to keep his job. But Cox was not quite able to beat out The Toe and instead became one of several fine players who just missed making the great Cleveland team. The Browns' coach, Paul Brown, knew these men could play for just about any other team in the league. He did not want to cut them from his team for fear they would join another top team and help to beat the Browns. So instead he traded them to the worst teams for a very low price. Cleveland sent Cox and three other players to the weak Minnesota Vikings in exchange for a mere sixth-round draft choice.

At the Vikings' camp, Fred again showed his talent. He smashed kickoffs into the end zone during the exhibition season and kicked field goals and extra points without a miss. But a few days later, Fred was dropped from the team. Poor Fred must have wondered just what it would take to convince people that he belonged in pro football. The Vikings, however, soon realized their mistake and in midseason cut the man they had kept in place of Fred. They sent word to Fred, who was teaching science back in Pennsylvania, that he would be welcome to try out again in 1963.

In 1963 Fred made certain that no one could ignore him. When he booted five straight field goals in his first exhibition game, Fred was rewarded with the job as the Vikings placekicker. But since the Vikings only wanted to keep one kicker, Cox was also stuck with the task of punting. Fortunately, he only had to punt one long year before someone else took over that part of his job.

It took Fred only a couple of years to become one of the best in the business of placekicking. In 1965 he led the league with 23 field goals. But Fred also had unpleasant days when he proved that he was only human. Fred's worst day came in 1967 against the Detroit Lions. That day it seemed almost as though his foot was on crooked because he missed four field goals. But games like that happened very rarely. In both 1969 and 1970, Fred led the entire conference in scoring. And although the 1970 Vikings were loaded with stars like Carl Eller and Alan Page, Fred was voted the team's Most Valuable Player that year.

It is rare today for a kicker to make all of his

Cox, who played in four Super Bowls, swings his leg into action.

points after touchdowns. For the Vikings, however, the extra point was almost automatic. From 1969 to 1973, Fred kicked 170 straight extra points through the uprights. Fred also managed to get himself involved in almost every game the Vikings played. And at 151 games, he still holds the National Football League record for consecutive games scoring. Once Cox even made a long field goal with a 40 mph wind blowing across the field. This also kept alive his other NFL record—kicking a field goal in 31 games in a row.

What made his statistics even more impressive was the fact that football was only a part-time job for Cox. While the other players would rest up on Monday after a game, Fred would be up early, studying to become a chiropractor. In fact, he ran his own clinic in Buffalo, Minnesota, during the last six years of his career. The Vikings thought so much of Cox that they let him work out his own schedule for getting in his practice kicks.

Towards the end of his career, Fred's valuable right leg lost some of its power. His kickoffs dropped so far short of the end zone that he tried a new method of kicking off. Instead of getting off a high kick, Fred would bounce it along the ground with plenty of spin. Viking fans were not impressed with those weak kicks even though they would often give kick returners problems.

The Viking coaches, however, were not so much concerned with how far Cox kicked the ball. They wanted someone who could stay calm and kick straight, even in tense situations. And no one was more calm than Fred. In many tight games, he would trot out for a last-second field goal while

On the sidelines, Fred waits for his call to enter the game.

the Viking fans, sitting on the edges of their seats, were screaming frantically. Amid all of the racket, Fred would be the same unemotional man his patients would see in the office the next day.

During his football career, Fred made 282 field goals and was ranked as one of the top five scorers in NFL history. He proved he was not only an expert on the treatment of the human back; he also knew the value of a strong leg.

Tom Dempsey, the record-setting kicker with only half a foot, watches one of his kicks sail toward the goalposts.

4
Tom Dempsey

In 1969 a New Orleans newspaper printed a photograph of Tom Dempsey kicking a 19-yard field goal to win the game for the New Orleans Saints. The average reader would have seen nothing unusual about the picture. However, anyone who knew Tom Dempsey must have been shocked to see the big kicker booting the ball with a *whole* right foot. Dempsey had been born with the front portion of his foot missing. But when the newspaper editor had seen the original picture of Dempsey, he thought there had been something wrong with the camera film. So he had one of his artists paint on the rest of the foot before printing the picture!

When Tom was growing up, there had been many days when he had wished that someone could fix his foot as easily as the artist had changed his

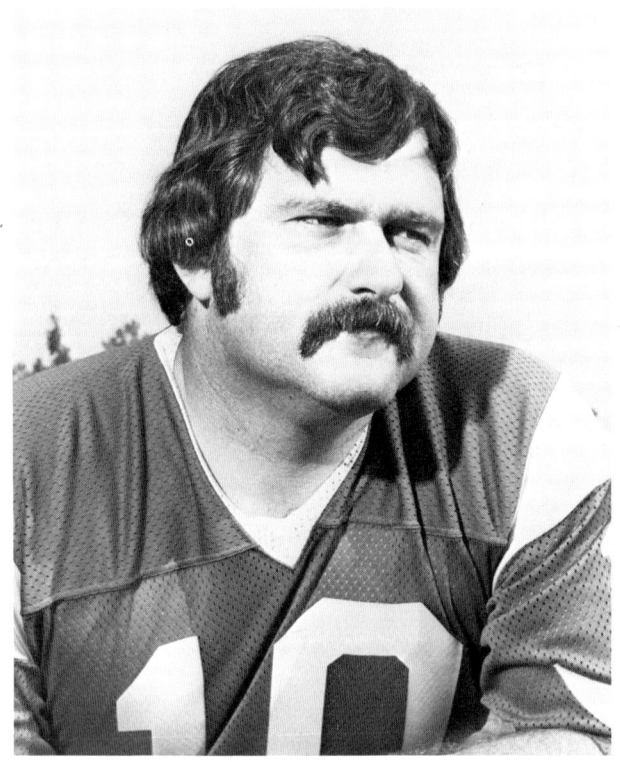

Tom Dempsey

photograph. He was born in Milwaukee, Wisconsin, in 1947, with several handicaps. Not only did he have no toes on his right foot, he also had no right hand and only a shriveled remainder of a forearm.

After moving to California at the age of two, Tom had 16 operations to try to improve his arm and foot. All of this time, Tom had to put up with the teasing from other children. At first the taunts made him feel as though he really were something strange and not at all like "normal people." But Dempsey's father sat down with him one day and convinced Tom that he was no different from anyone else. If he wanted, his father said, he could do anything that his friends could. To prove his point, Tom's father played all kinds of sports with him.

Tom quickly learned that he *could* play and work as well as anyone else. When he was in high school, he made believers out of his opponents in football and wrestling. And although the challenge of playing on the college level was even stiffer, Tom again excelled. At Palomar Junior College in California, he was voted to the all-conference team as a defensive end. When he was not blasting opposing linemen with his 260-pound body, Tom went out for other sports. He continued to wrestle and even put the shot 50 feet for the track team.

It was at Palomar Junior College that Tom discovered placekicking. He found that his light, stubby foot could whip into the ball at a faster speed than most kickers. And because his foot was always locked stiff, Tom did not have to worry about it slipping or wobbling as he swung. There was one disadvantage, however. Tom's foot, like the short barrel of a gun, was less accurate than a longer foot would be.

After college Tom tried out with the San Diego Chargers in 1968, but he did not win a spot on the team. The next season, however, he caught on with the New Orleans Saints and provided New Orleans' fans with some of the few bright moments in their history. Equipped with a special, wedge-shaped shoe, Tom made 61 percent of his field goal tries his first season. His 22 field goals and 33 extra-point kicks gave him 99 points, one of the top-scoring marks in the league. The big rookie so impressed people that he was named to the Pro Bowl game that first year in the pros.

The next season Dempsey earned a spot in the record book that has lasted for more than 10 years. In a game in New Orleans, the Saints were struggling to stay close to the Detroit Lions. The Saints trailed, 17-16, and only Dempsey's three field goals had kept his team within range. In the closing seconds, New Orleans was bottled up back in their own end of the field, and there was only time for one last, hopeless play. In that situation, most teams would throw the ball far down field and hope for a lucky catch or a penalty.

The Lions, then, could hardly believe it when the Saints sent in their field goal unit. Some Saints later claimed that their coach had mistakenly thought

Tom Dempsey kicks his record-breaking 63-yard field goal to beat Detroit on November 8, 1970.

the ball was on the Lions' 45-yard line instead of the Saints' 45, or he might not have tried the kick. As it was, the ball sat 55 yards away from the goal line. Dempsey had his holder crouch 8 yards beyond the line of scrimmage so that the kick would not be blocked.

When the center snapped the ball, the Lions charged halfheartedly, expecting some kind of a trick play. Tom swung his powerful leg into the ball, and players on both teams turned to watch the flight of the ball. The ball looked so tiny as it sailed far away toward the goalposts, but the roar of the crowd revealed the incredible news. Tom's 63-yard kick had won the game, 19-17! And Dempsey had smashed the record that had been held by Baltimore's Bert Rechichar since 1956!

But Tom was soon to find out that being a placekicker was like being a drummer in a band. If you played well, people couldn't help but notice you. But if you make a mistake, *everyone* noticed you even more. And in 1971 Tom was making mistakes. His troubles were not helped by his new coach who insisted that Tom lose weight—and quickly. At that time, Tom was no heavier than he had been the year before, so the coach's criticism bothered him. Then when Tom began to miss field goals during the exhibition season, kickers flocked to the Saints' camp, eager to take over. At one point, nearly 20 placekickers went after Tom's job. In the end, one of them beat Dempsey out for a spot on the team.

Less than a year after setting his marvelous record, Dempsey was unwanted. Although he was discouraged, he still went out to a park at night to practice his kicking. It was hard work chasing each ball himself, but he stayed with it.

Dempsey and his Los Angeles Ram holder walk off the field.

Finally the call came from the Philadelphia Eagles. They remembered how well Tom had kicked as a rookie, and in 1971 they signed him to a contract. That season Tom not only sent kicks booming from long range, he also led the league in field goal accuracy.

Dempsey kicked well for the Eagles until 1975. But when the Eagles learned that the poor-kicking Los Angeles Rams were willing to give up a fourth round draft choice for Tom, the Eagles traded him away.

41

Dempsey rips into one for the Buffalo Bills.

Tom soon proved to the Rams that he still had some good kicks left in him. He made 21 field goals in 26 tries, a fine percentage. But the Rams had become convinced that Dempsey's kicks were too low, and as a result, too easily blocked. After Tom left the Rams, he enjoyed brief appearances with the Houston Oilers and the Buffalo Bills.

Although Tom's stay in the National Football League was fairly short compared to most top kickers, it was certainly memorable. And Tom has been admired for his efforts both on and off the field. Ten years after his famous kick, his 63-yard distance had not yet been equaled. Many have also said that Dempsey's courage in overcoming his handicaps has not been equaled either. Tom, of course, would disagree. Like his father had always told him, he had always believed that he was no different from any "normal" person. But as far as placekicking went, he was quite a bit better.

Garo Yepremian doesn't wait for the official to tell him his kick is good!

5
Garo Yepremian

All-pro tackle Alex Karras of the Detroit Lions was disgusted with what was happening in pro football. While the men who had grown up with the game and had learned it all of their lives banged heads at midfield, it was the kickers who were deciding the outcome of the games. Many of these placekickers were foreign soccer players who did not know the first thing about American football. Karras drew many laughs imitating these kickers. "I think I kick a touchdown," he would say. He made it clear he did not think these players belonged in the game.

Karras' Detroit teammate Garo Yepremian took the criticism good-naturedly. Garo was a perfect example of what Karras was talking about. He was wearing a pro football uniform before he knew

Garo Yepremian

much about the game at all. But the fact was that Garo could kick a football farther and straighter than nearly anyone else. As long as he did his job, his coach did not care if he had ever heard about the planet Earth, much less about football.

Garo's full name was Garabed Sarkis Yepremian. He was born in 1944 in Larnaca, Cyprus, an island in the Mediterranean Sea between Greece and Turkey. Garo attended a private school where he learned English and had excellent soccer instructors. Then at the age of 15, Garo moved with his family to England and found work in a clothing factory. It was not until he was 22 that Garo came to the United States and settled in Frankton, Indiana.

Garo's brother Krikor was already living in the United States when Garo arrived. Krikor was familiar with the story of a kicker for the Buffalo Bills, Pete Gogolak. The Gogolak family had fled to the United States from Hungary during an uprising there in 1956. In the United States, Pete soon found that his soccer style of kicking worked just as well with a football as it had with a soccer ball. In a soccer kick, players do not step into the ball and hit it head on with their toes. Instead they charge in from the side. Then they whip their foot around and kick the ball with the inside of the foot. After Gogolak joined the Buffalo Bills in 1964 and led the league in scoring, more teams started looking for soccer-style kickers. Krikor knew about Garo's soccer skill. He helped Garo write to several pro football clubs to ask them for a chance to show what he could do.

Garo's letters paid off, and in 1966 he was invited to try out for the Atlanta Falcons. In Atlanta he was right on target and hit 18 of 20 field goal tries. But while the Falcons were making up their minds about Yepremian, he signed the very next day with the Detroit Lions.

Yepremian, naturally, found his new surroundings quite strange. He tried to get people to quit asking him questions until he became more familiar with American football. He would politely tell people he did not speak English, but very few believed him because he gave the sentence in perfect English!

Despite the sneers from Karras and others, Garo made friends with his new teammates. He was a friendly, likeable fellow. And it certainly did not hurt when he kicked six field goals in a single game against the Minnesota Vikings that year!

Competition among kickers was always fierce, and in 1968 the Lions cut Garo. They decided the straight-ahead kicker, Errol Mann, was more reliable than the sidewinding Yepremian.

For a while Garo sat around feeling miserable. But then he thought what had worked once would work again, and he started writing letters to pro teams. While waiting for answers, he put his clothing factory experience to use making neckties.

In 1970 the Miami Dolphins invited Garo to training camp. At first they chose Karl Kremser over Garo as their kicker. But one game into the season, Garo was asked to take over. That season marked the beginning of success for both Yepremian and the Dolphins.

The shakiest moment in Garo's career with Miami came exactly one year after his first game as a Dolphin. In the opening game of 1971, Garo needed to make just one field goal to beat the Denver Broncos. But he missed *three* different times. Garo did not give up, however. The next week against the Buffalo Bills, he went out and booted five perfect field goal kicks for his team. Yepremian went on to lead the league in scoring that year with 117 points. Then in the AFC play-off game against the Kansas City Chiefs, Garo's 37-yard field goal ended the NFL's longest game in a 27-24 victory in the second quarter of overtime. Miami made it all the way to the Super Bowl, but they were beaten by the Dallas Cowboys. Yepremian scored the only Dolphin points in a 24-3 loss.

Compared to his Dolphin teammates, Garo looked like a small boy. Someone once asked him why he wore the number "1" on his uniform. Garo smiled and said it was about the only number he had room for on his back! He stood 5 feet, 7 inches tall and weighed only about 165 pounds. With his small size and balding head, he seemed like the last person to belong on a pro football field.

One of the few left-footed kickers in the game, Yepremian uses the sidewinding, soccer-style approach to put the ball through the uprights.

Unfortunately in a Super Bowl game in front of millions of fans, he proved just how little he actually did know about football.

In 1972 the Dolphins had raced through the season and the play-offs without losing a game. Then in the Super Bowl, the Washington Redskins were finding they had no better luck against Miami than anyone else. The Dolphins grabbed a 14-0 lead and threatened to add to it, moving the ball deep into Redskin territory. With just seven minutes left in the contest, a field goal would put the game safely out of reach.

Garo lined up for a 43-yard attempt. The kick was low and was blocked at the line of scrimmage. The football bounced back and landed in Garo's hands. He started to run with the ball until he saw large, mean-looking Redskins bearing down on him. That made Garo do what any normal person would have done—he panicked! He tried to get rid of the ball, but he only managed to flip it straight up in the air. Washington's Mike Bass grabbed the ball and raced downfield, untouched. Suddenly Miami's safe lead was cut to 14-7. Fortunately, the Miami defense held on to the lead, and Yepremian could later laugh about his big moment.

Leaving the passing to others, Garo continued to kick well for the Dolphins until 1979. Just the previous year, 1978, he had started an amazing streak and had ended the season with 17 straight field goals without a miss. That was just one short of breaking the league record for consecutive field goals. It was a very unlucky time for Yepremian to lose his job, but the Dolphins dropped the 35-year old from the team in favor of the younger, stronger Uwe Von Schaumann.

Garo spent the next several weeks sitting in the stands, wondering if he would ever get a chance to break the field goal record. Then in midseason, his chance came. When the New Orleans Saints lost their top kicker with a leg injury, Garo happily answered their call for help. He soon stretched his streak to 20 field goals before finally missing.

At the end of the season, New Orleans, too, replaced Garo with a younger kicker. But at this point in his career, he no longer had to write letters to teams. The Tampa Bay Buccaneers eagerly signed him to a contract, and that season Garo became one of the only nine NFL kickers to have kicked 200 or more field goals. When he set that record, Garo again proved that he was still one of the top kickers in football history.

Yepremian steps into one for the Tampa Bay Buccaneers.

Efren Herrera and holder Jim Zorn watch a Herrera kick travel toward the end zone.

6
Efren Herrera

The high, booming kick is the trademark of most of football's top placekickers. Efren Herrera is, however, just as well known for his little taps that tumble crazily like a jumping bean for 15 yards. Not that Herrera is not capable of booting a long, high kick when the time is right. It's just that Efren knows there is also a place in pro football for a controlled, short kick. And Herrera has shown that he can do more valuable things with a football than any other kicker in the game.

Efren was born in Guadalajara, Mexico, in 1951. The streets of his hometown were often buzzing with pick-up soccer games, and Efren joined in these games when he was only four years old.

Efren soon began to master the skills of kicking a soccer ball, but it seemed that he would never get the chance to use them. Because his family was poor, his father insisted that Efren start working for a living as soon as possible. So Efren dropped out of high school to work in an automobile body shop. At first he enjoyed working with cars. But after a year and a half, Herrera longed to do something else.

It was then that Efren decided to live with a sister in West Covina, California, and to continue his schooling. For a while, life in the United States was difficult for him, because he knew practically no English and had trouble communicating with English-speaking people. Each morning he also had to walk six miles to La Puenta High School because the nearby school would not accept him.

Herrera often stayed late at the high school to work out with the cross-country team. During one workout, he found a basketball laying in the grass. He was warned not to kick it, but he could not resist booting the ball toward the goalposts.

When Efren was called into the coach's office the next day, he thought he would be scolded for kicking the ball. While the coach had found out about Herrera kicking the basketball, he was not angry. Instead the coach asked Efren if he could kick a football as well as he could kick a basketball!

When Efren set out to prove that he could kick a football even farther, all of his kicks sailed perfectly straight. But they all went *under* the crossbar. Herrera had thought that football was played like soccer, and in soccer the ball was kicked under the bar to score a goal. After much confusion, the coach was finally able to convince Efren to kick the ball *over* the bar.

In high school Herrera quickly developed into a fine kicker and a hard-hitting safety as well. Then in 1970 he went on to college at the University of California at Los Angeles (UCLA). By his sophomore year, Efren had won the regular placekicking job and was on his way to breaking 10 UCLA kicking records. One of the highlights of his college career came in a 1972 game against the University of Nebraska. In that game Efren kicked a 30-yard field goal in the final minute of play to defeat the defending national champions.

After winning All-American honors in 1973 from *The Sporting News,* Efren was claimed by the Detroit Lions on the seventh round of the 1974 draft. But he lasted only a few weeks before the Lions cut him. But a month later, the Dallas Cowboys gave Herrera a second chance. This time he replaced former Austrian soccer star, Toni

Herrera was one of the league's most accurate kickers when he played for the Dallas Cowboys.

Fritsch, as the Cowboys' regular kicker. That season Efren made 8 of 13 field goals and was perfect on extra points.

After sitting out the 1975 season with a knee injury, Efren returned to the Cowboys, stronger than ever. In 1976 he was again perfect on extra points, and he tied New Orleans' Rich Szaro for the league's best field goal percentage with 78 percent. The following year, Herrera's 62 percent field goal record was again tops in the conference, as was his point total of 93. Herrera's bull's-eye kicks also helped the Cowboys to win the 1978 Super Bowl when they defeated Denver, 27-10.

Herrera's kicking style was unique. Most soccer-style kickers took two or three steps before kicking and swung their leg across their body. Efren took only one step and then he drove his leg toward the target. Because he took only one step, Herrera's kicks got off the ground quickly and there was little chance of one of them being blocked. Experts decided that Efren's accurate, low-risk kicks had made him the best kicker in the league that year.

The Dallas Cowboys, unfortunately, did not agree with Efren about how valuable he was. So when they did not pay him what he wanted, he refused to play for them in 1978. Finally the Cowboys traded Efren to the Seattle Seahawks for a fifth-round draft choice.

Trading for Herrera turned out to be one of the Seahawks' better moves. In his first season with Seattle, Efren beat two powerful teams with last-minute field goals. He chipped the ball through the goalposts from 19 yards to beat the Minnesota Vikings, and he kicked a 46-yarder to defeat the Oakland Raiders.

Waiting for the snap from center, Herrera concentrates on the spot where Jim Zorn will place the ball for the kick.

In 1979 Efren scored a career-high 100 points. He was locked in a furious battle for the top kicking percentage in the league with Toni Fritsch, who was now with the Houston Oilers. Fritsch finally won with 84 percent while Herrera—with longer, more difficult attempts—finished with 82 percent.

The Seahawks, however, were not content to limit Efren to kicking field goals. They found he could also add a few more weapons to Seattle's wild, high-scoring offense. One of these was the on-side kick. In football a kickoff that travels at least 10 yards is a free ball, and whoever recovers it goes on offense. It is usually risky to try an intentionally short kick, or "on-side" kick, because the kicking team rarely recovers the ball and has to give up a good field position. But Efren placed his kicks so carefully that in 1979 Seattle recovered three of four attempts. Once Efren tapped the ball and roared after it himself. Football fans, who were used to kickers avoiding contact, were amazed when Efren outscrambled everyone to recover his own kick!

In one game against the Atlanta Falcons, the Seahawks also used Herrera as a secret weapon on a fake field goal. Seattle lined up for the kick, and Efren started forward to kick the ball. At the last instant, holder Jim Zorn pulled the ball away and stood up, and Efren ducked through a wall of blockers and ran downfield. He was wide open when Zorn tossed the ball to him for a Seattle first down.

Herrera also gave the Seahawks an extra tackler on kickoffs. He enjoyed hurling his 5-foot, 9-inch, 190-pound body into pile-ups to help bring down ballcarriers. While the Seahawks hoped Herrera would not get too carried away with his enthusiasm, they found it was hard to stop him from proving that he was the best all-around kicker in football.

7
Rolf Benirschke

On November 12, 1979, the Pittsburgh Steelers were preparing to thrash yet another victim. In the four previous weeks, the awesome Steelers had battered four good teams—the Dallas Cowboys, the Denver Broncos, the Washington Redskins, and the Kansas City Chiefs—and all by lop-sided scores. Now the television network was hoping that a strong San Diego team could keep that game from becoming another boring Pittsburgh romp.

Just before the game, the Chargers' captains for the game were introduced to the home crowd. One of them, Rolf Benirschke, tottered weakly out on to the field. Alongside 280-pound defensive tackle Lou Kelcher, who weighed over twice as much as Rolf, he looked like a skeleton.

Rolf Benirschke

The crowd thundered applause down on their Charger hero. They knew that Rolf would not be playing that day. Few people, in fact, had ever expected to see him play again. But they were happy just to see him alive and on his feet.

The TV network was disappointed once again, because almost from the very start the game was no contest. This time, however, it was the Steelers who were being run out of the stadium. Inspired by their beanpole kicker, Benirschke, the Chargers pounded Pittsburgh, 35-7.

Rolf Joachim Benirschke had always been treated warmly by San Diego fans. Although he was born in Boston in 1955, Rolf was a hometown hero in San Diego. When Rolf was young, his family had moved west, and he had played high school ball in nearby LaJolla, California. From there it had been just a short jump to the University of California at Davis. Rolf, who had always been an animal lover, studied zoology at college. And in his spare time, he put his powerful right leg to work in both soccer and football.

Rolf's placekicking for Cal-Davis impressed the pro scouts, but just barely. Benirschke nearly won the humble honor of being the last person chosen in the entire 1977 college player draft. The Oakland Raiders, with the second-to-last pick, finally selected Rolf.

That year in training camp, the young kicker gave the Raiders no reason to change their opinion of him. But when they dropped Rolf from the team, the San Diego Chargers picked him up. The Chargers felt they had nothing to lose by giving the local ballplayer a chance.

The Chargers, however, certainly could not have expected Rolf to come through as well as he did. With his soccer style of kicking, Benirschke was

Benirschke attempts to launch a kick over the outstretched arms of a Steeler defender.

so deadly at short range that the Chargers kept him as their regular placekicker. Quickly but quietly, Rolf was becoming one of the most accurate kickers in pro football. Even when he began feeling mysterious stomach cramps in 1978, he kept zeroing in on the goalposts. That year Rolf booted 18 of 22 field goal tries for his team for an amazing record of 82 percent.

By the start of the 1979 season, Rolf's cramps had gotten worse. Doctors were puzzled by his illness and suspected that it was a form of Crohn's disease. Although doctors knew it was a condition of the intestines, no one knew what caused the disease or what could be done about it. So Rolf decided he would just play with the pain, and he continued his remarkable string of successful kicks. By the end of the season's fourth game, which San Diego lost to New England, he had made 13 straight field goals. After that game, Benirschke fell violently ill with a temperature of 105 degrees and was rushed to the hospital. One operation was needed right away in order to save his life, and he had to have another operation four days later.

Even after his operations, the likeable young man was still in serious trouble. His 6-foot, 170-pound frame, oddly thin for a football player, had wasted away to 125 pounds. As Rolf lay in intensive care at the hospital for two weeks, the pains and fever hurt so much that he did not really want to live. Rolf's father was a doctor, and when Rolf saw the worried looks on his father's face, he knew that his family was very concerned about him. It was when Benirschke's hundreds of fans lined up at the stadium to offer to donate blood that he realized he had many friends. And then he started to fight back against his illness.

At first Rolf set simple goals for himself. He was determined to get up off his back, then to get out of bed, and then to try to walk. By the time of the Pittsburgh game, Rolf had just gotten back on his feet. That day the cheers of the crowd and the excitement of seeing his teammates beat the Super Bowl champs gave him a new goal. He decided he would not only recover from his illness. He would also play for the Chargers again.

This time, as before, the work was slow. At first Rolf could only use three-pound weights for his strength exercises. Because a football was too heavy for him to kick, he practiced with a soccer ball.

When the Chargers' summer camp opened the following season, Benirschke surprised his coaches by showing up. But although they admired the young man, they would not just give Rolf's job back to him. Mike Wood, who had replaced Benirschke in 1979, had been almost perfect in his field-goal kicking, so Rolf would have to beat him out for the spot. But as the training camp went on, Rolf showed he was even stronger and better than he had been before his illness. He soon earned the

The ball is placed on the turf as Benirschke steps up for a kick. In 1980, Rolf scored 118 points, second highest in the NFL.

placekicking job for San Diego and picked up right where he had left off.

That year Rolf ran his streak of field goals to 16 without a miss before he finally missed one.

One of the field goals was a 52-yard kick that helped the Chargers to beat the Oakland Raiders. From the season's first game, Rolf found himself among the AFC scoring leaders.

When the Chargers' kickoff man was hurt early in the season, Rolf volunteered to take over the chores. Coach Don Coryell fretted over his decision for a while. He knew how dangerous it was for players even far more powerful than Benirschke to wander in among the flying bodies of a kickoff return. Coryell finally told Rolf that he could kick off if he promised to run straight to the bench after kicking. For a pro team to play short one man rather than risk an injury to their star kicker, was a real tribute to Rolf Benirschke, the 1980 comeback player of the year.

8
Tony Franklin

The hot summer sun baking down in Big Spring, Texas, did not stop young Tony Franklin from running around outdoors. But it gave him a good reason to get rid of his shoes and to go barefoot. Even when it came to kicking games, Tony and his childhood friends could not be bothered with wearing shoes. Instead with their bare feet they took turns kicking a football over an old swing set.

Several years later, Franklin found himself playing kicking games again, although he would much rather have been a running back than a place-kicker. During his freshman year in high school, the little 5-foot, 8-inch, 175 pounder had gained more than 1,500 yards running. But later that same year, he had twisted his ankle so badly that it had to be put in a cast. With the heavy cast weighing down his foot, Tony couldn't run at all for a while. But he enjoyed football so much that he did not want to drop out. When Tony noticed the team's kicker having troubles, he decided to practice kicking himself. His injury did not bother him too much and Franklin was able to step head on into the ball and boot it about 30 yards. But even for a high school boy, that was a pretty short range.

One day Franklin happened to see the Kansas City Chiefs in a pro football game. The Chiefs' kicker was Jan Stenerud, the college ski-jumping champion from Norway. During the game, Stenerud rushed at the ball from the side and whipped his leg around from the side. When Tony went out afterwards and tried Stenerud's soccer style of kicking, he found that he could get an extra ten yards.

But 40 yards was still only an average distance for a kicker. It was only when Franklin remembered the old days of kicking the ball barefoot over the swing that his kicking became extraordinary. Just as an experiment, Tony took off his shoe before one of his kicks. For some reason, the kick went sailing even 10 yards further than before!

Tony Franklin's bare foot has kicked some of the longest field goals in football.

After that incident, Tony wore only a sock on his kicking foot throughout high school. Before he graduated from high school in 1975, he had shocked his coaches with a 58-yard field goal. Very few *pros* had ever kicked one so far!

That autumn Franklin brought his famous right foot to Texas A&M University. But because there was an unusual amount of rain that season, Tony had problems. The sock on his kicking foot kept getting waterlogged. Tony finally grew tired of changing his wet socks and decided to kick barefoot instead.

While Tony was at Texas A&M, the kickers in his conference suddenly began to boot the ball almost out of sight. Arkansas' Steve Little, Texas' Russell Erxleben, and Franklin were connecting on so many long-range bombs that it was ridiculous. During his junior year, Tony broke the pro and college record *twice* in a single game when he sent the ball over the crossbar from 64 and 65 yards!

When Erxleben, a powerful, straight-ahead kicker, took up Franklin's challenge, he kicked a mighty 67-yarder to take away Tony's record. College coaches wondered how much farther these two could go in their rivalry. It turned out that neither

Tony Franklin

could top the 67-yard mark during a game. But Tony made a kick in practice that was almost frightening. His coach bet him a cigar that he could not make one out of three attempts from 76 yards. Normally that would be the safest bet in the world. But the coach looked on nervously as Tony just missed one to the left and one a few feet to the right. On his third kick, Tony drilled it over the bar and won his cigar.

Although Franklin had set 18 college records for kicking, the pros were far more impressed with Erxleben, who was also a top punter. The University of Texas kicker was one of the first players chosen in the 1979 college draft, while Franklin was not claimed by the Philadelphia Eagles until the third round. The Eagles had suffered from poor placekicking in previous years, and they had even lost a play-off game in 1978 on a missed kick.

Now with Tony as their kicker, the Eagles became a threat to score every time they crossed midfield. Some college kickers had trouble in switching to pro ball because a kicking block wasn't allowed for field goals. But Tony had an easy adjustment because of his unique kicking skills. As the only barefoot kicker in the league, Tony made sure that his team scored at least three points whenever they got close to the end zone.

In a nationally televised game against their arch rival, the Dallas Cowboys, the Eagle offense bogged down at the Dallas 42-yard line. The Eagles' coach added on 7 yards to where the placeholder would have to crouch and then 10 more as the goal posts were 10 yards behind the goal line. When the coach asked Franklin if he could make the

Even after he has kicked the ball, Franklin keeps his head down as he completes his follow-through.

kick, Franklin could hardly wait to show him that he could. He then ran out and kicked the 59 yarder straight through the middle of the goal posts. Tony's kick was a great boost to the Eagles, who went on to win the game, 31-21.

Later in the season, the weather grew cold in the northern cities of the league. Tony had never had to worry about freezing weather before, but

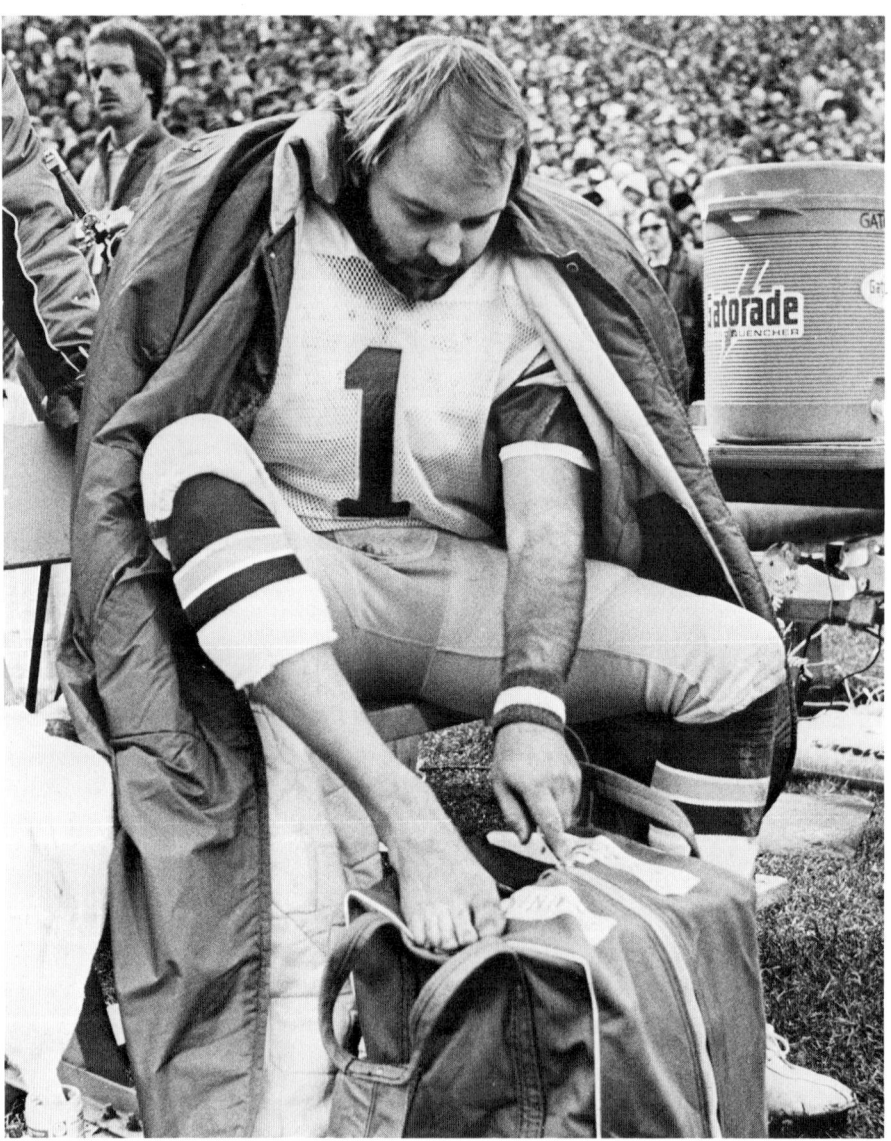
Franklin warms his kicking foot on the sidelines. On cold days, opposing coaches have called time out just before a Franklin field goal try. They hope to chill him into missing the three-pointer.

he still refused to wear a shoe. Instead he stood on the sidelines with his foot stuffed into a padded foot warmer. Then when it came time to kick his foot was warm, and his kicking was just as accurate as ever.

Tony's 59-yard field goal in the Dallas game was the longest in the league that year. He also kicked 22 other field goals and made 20 of 24 from inside 50 yards. In all he totaled 105 points, which was one of the best records in the league. Franklin also helped out on kickoffs. His high, floating kicks would often hang in the air longer than four seconds. This would give the Eagles plenty of time to race downfield and surround the returner.

Unfortunately, the peppy rookie finished his spectacular first year on a sour note. In a play-off game against the Tampa Bay Buccaneers, the Eagles fell far behind early in the game. But in the last quarter, Philadelphia moved back to within a touchdown of the Bucs. Tony's coach told him to kick the ball deep. There was still enough time left in the game for the Eagles to stop Tampa, forcing them to punt, and to get the ball in a good field position. Instead Franklin tried a short on-side kick and hoped that one of his teammates could recover the ball. The kick failed, and Tampa, instead of being deep in their own end of the field, had the ball around midfield. That made the Eagles' task too difficult, and they ran out of time before they could come up with a score.

Although the Philadelphia coaches were angry with Franklin after the Tampa game, more often than not the little kicker would bring smiles to their faces. And his long, accurate kicks will give the Eagles an extra edge in their bid to become the NFL champions of the 1980s.

ACKNOWLEDGMENTS: The photographs are reproduced through the courtesy of: pp. 4, 54, 60, Seattle Seahawks; pp. 7, 26, 31, 33, Minnesota Vikings; pp. 10, 13, Cleveland Browns; pp. 16, 21, 25, Oakland Raiders; p. 24, Chicago Bears; pp. 34, 36, 41, Los Angeles Rams; pp. 34, 44, New Orleans Saints; p. 42, Buffalo Bills, Robert L. Smith Photography; pp. 46, 50, Miami Dolphins; p. 53, Tampa Bay Buccaneers; p. 58, Dallas Cowboys; p. 64, San Diego Chargers; p. 66, San Diego Chargers, Russ Gilbert Photo; p. 69, San Diego Chargers, Tony De Palmer Photo; pp. 73, 77, Philadelphia Eagles, Ed Mahan Photo; p. 75, Philadelphia Eagles; p. 78, Vernon J. Biever Photo.

Cover photograph: Vernon J. Biever